# FROM AUTHOR TO ENTREPRENEUR

How to Turn Your Book into a Business

## Julia A Royston

BK Royston Publishing
P. O. Box 4321
Jeffersonville, IN  47131
502-802-5385
http://www.bkroystonpublishing.com
bkroystonpublishing@gmail.com

© Copyright – 2018

All Rights Reserved.  No part of this book may be reproduced, stored in a retrieval system, or transmitted by any means without the written permission of the author.

Cover Design:  Richetta Blackmon for Virtually Splendid – virtuallysplendid@gmail.com

ISBN: 978-1-946111-52-4



Printed in the United States of America

# DEDICATION

I dedicate this book to anyone who has written a book but realizes that your book is so much more.

I also dedicate this book to every author who has written a book but it hasn't given you the results that you thought. Let these words breathe life back into your book for you to release it again with a new understanding of what it takes to go from "Author to Entrepreneur."

# ACKNOWLEDGMENTS

First, I acknowledge my Lord and Savior Jesus Christ for giving me all of my gifts and especially my gift to write His words.

My husband who is always supportive, loving and encouraging me to utilize all of my gifts and talents. Thank you honey.

To my mother, Dr. Daisy Foree, who is my number one cheerleader and always tells me, "hang in there, you can do it." To my father, Dr. Jack Foree, who is never far away from me in my spirit, heart or face. I only have to look in the mirror each day to see him.

To Rev. Claude and Mrs. Lillie Royston who support me in everything I do.

To the rest of my family, I love you and thank you for your prayers, support and love.

To my great friend Vanessa Collins who is always encouraging me to write and try new things in my business. Thanks for being there with me every step of the way. God brought into my life for such a time as this. Love you.

To my business Coach, Dawniel P. Winningham, who has challenged me to be better, go further and do more than I ever thought I would in business.

To my BK Royston Publishing, Royal Media and Publishing and Writing Coaching community of authors, graphic designers and future publishers, I thank you and love you. Let's go!

Julia Royston

# Table of Contents

| | |
|---|---|
| DEDICATIONS | iii |
| ACKNOWLEDGMENTS | v |
| INTRODUCTION | ix |
| BUSINESS IS IN MY BLOOD, WHAT'S IN YOURS? | 1 |
| IT STARTS WITH YOU | 7 |
| MIND, BODY AND SOUL | 17 |
| THE BOOK | 33 |
| PRODUCTS AND SERVICES | 45 |
| SYSTEMS | 65 |
| THE DREAM TEAM | 91 |
| THE ACTION PLAN | 101 |
| LESSONS LEARNED | 107 |
| ABOUT THE AUTHOR | 113 |

# Introduction

In 1994, I went through a divorce while simultaneously attending graduate school. It truly was the worst and best time in my life. Fortunately for me, I had the most supportive family ever, great guidance from professors and a part-time job with lawyers. The lawyers took care of the divorce situation, while I concentrated on finishing my degree. After graduation in August of 1994, I started doing something that I had never done before; journaling. Journaling to me was private. It was the first time that I would put my thoughts on paper and not be judged or have it graded by a professor. It was freeing and liberating to say the least. I found a way to release my emotions, express myself with a whole new art form and eventually heal. Who knew this same girl would come to love writing after my 5th-grade teacher had thrown a handwriting book at me years earlier, and told me that I had horrible handwriting. I misunderstood what she said, classified myself as a horrible writer and left off the handwriting part. I spent years not believing that I wrote well enough for a paper let alone a dissertation or more than 35 books. Sometimes you have to prove others wrong by just doing it. That's eventually what I did.

    Fast forward to 2006. A new man, new job, new state and new life. It was now time to pull out all of those 80-page spiral notebooks filled with my personal thoughts, feelings and writings to be compiled for the world to see. Why? Because God said it was time to write the book. I thought what book? He said those notebooks that you've been writing in for years; get them out, type them up and compile them into a book. I didn't have a clue. I don't normally argue with

God. I question, try hard to resist and pray hard about what He said, but eventually, He wins.

It was my first book and it was poetry. Not a book filled with man-bashing, but the book was filled with heartfelt poetry. I was proud of it. I even created a one-woman show around it and combined my music with my poetry and produced a live CD/DVD. It was my first combined set or bundle of products that I put together. Oh wow. People in the audience loved it and received a copy of the book with their entry into the recording which included a dinner buffet. It was awesome. I felt like a big-time artist. Me, a musician and the microphone. It was raw, up close and personal.

I kept writing and created a devotional book about how much God loves us and 30 ways that He is still loving us with his protection, love and care today. I was proud of that book as well. I traveled around the city, region and nation with my music and books. It was incredible. At the height of my travels, I had as many as 90 events a year. Yes, there are only 52 weeks in the year. In some weekends, I had as many as 4 events, because I could attend 2 on Saturdays and 2 services on Sundays. It was an incredible and tiring experience to say the least. Don't judge me! I was young and filled with energy.

In 2009, something happened that would change everything. I was attending a conference event as a vendor. I had my books, music CDs, business cards, a swiper machine for credit cards and a smile. I was ready to meet and greet anyone who came near my table for possible sales. I have always been an extrovert and love meeting new people. There was a young woman who was an acquaintance of mine who I had seen at multiple events, and she stopped by to say hello. We talked for a minute and then she said, "I want you to publish my book because I write poetry." I knew that she was not only a praise dancer but the leader of the praise dance ministry at her church.

I said, "You want me to tell you or teach you how I did it?"

She said, "No, I don't want to learn. I am going to pay you money to put together my book of poetry. Let's meet! You tell me how much, and I will pay you to publish my book."

I had been asked before if I ever published other people's books beside my own and had declined. But this was someone that I liked. She offered to pay me upfront without a price quote, and I wanted to help her. I really just wanted to only publish her one book. I had not planned on publishing anyone's books but my own. Really. I am being honest here. I just wanted my company or business name to protect my books.

I was sure that she would be the only person's book that I would publish, so it was okay, right? Wrong! There was much, more to come. There were more people to meet, more decisions to make and much more learning that had to take place to actually have a business; any business and especially the publishing business. Needless to say; I did it, and she loved it. Great! I'm glad she loved and was proud of my work. The only problem was; when people asked her who published her book, she didn't say a friend, but me! She became my first referral to other people in her very large church that I was her publisher. I tried to minimize my role as a publisher, but it didn't work. When people asked how much I would charge to publish their book, I quoted a price and they said yes. I had to make a decision. Was I in business or not? My husband was on board especially when additional income came in our home. I realized that it was something that I could do and was now being recommended by someone to others that I did this well. I finally agreed. I was now in the publishing business.

Fast forward to the present, and I have now have signed to date more than 75+ authors and published 150+ books. I use the "+" sign because there are always books in production and new authors that I meet or speak to on a daily basis. Over the years; I realize that the book is not only the new business card, but the book is a business.

When you publish a book, you are now in the "book business." Sure you may or may not be signed to a publishing company; but when your name is on the front cover of a hard copy book or on the image of an eBook, you are a part of the publishing, book and literary industry. You help keep the industry alive and thriving. Your sales that are generated on a distribution site are now recorded. Your book cover can be seen and purchased by millions around the world if you have online distribution. You can profit from your book in multiple ways including on your own site. You are a part of the statistics of new books released; especially, if your book is available on Amazon, Barnes & Noble, KINDLE, NOOK or KOBO or any of the new distribution outlet sites for books.

I have been sharing with authors, motivational speakers, ministry leaders, non-profit leaders and coaches around the world how they can write a book that can accompany their businesses. I now want to tell you how to turn that one book that you are thinking about writing or have handwritten notes on napkins or paper towels or scribbled down hardly readable ideas in notebooks hidden in your nightstand or boxed in storage, into a profitable business. Yes, really?

Anything you attempt won't always be easy. But with a guide, mentor or coach, the process will be clearer, and you will avoid some of the mistakes, pitfalls and wrong decisions that I made along the way.

If you desire to reach out to me throughout any part of this process, don't hesitate to visit http://bit.ly/talkwithroyston and let's talk, focus and strategize! Until then, get your seatbelt tightened, get your creative hat on and Let's Go!

# FROM AUTHOR TO ENTREPRENEUR

# Business is in my Blood. What's in Yours?

I struggled and debated how I should start this book. I wanted to start with the book because that is my passion. I love to write, love the creative process, etc. but realize that everything doesn't start with the book. The real place to begin to turn your book into a business starts with you.

Business is in my blood, and using multiple gifts to produce money comes from both sides of my family. My mother and father's fathers worked multiple jobs. My father's father could do multiple things, and he had the personality and work ethic to do it. He also raised 7 children, so he had to. He was a tobacco sharecropper which was extremely hard work, but only an annual payday. So, what did he do until harvest time?  He cleaned houses.  He picked vegetables. He painted houses in the summer because he and his brothers painted our house seemingly every year.  My dad wanted to support his father even after he left home.  My grandfather did all types of work including be a waiter during the Kentucky Derby Season which is huge in the state of Kentucky. There was no legal job that he could do, that he wasn't willing to do and do it well.  My grandfather, Jesse Foree, Sr. could do a lot because he did a lot.  I know that sounds confusing. But when you can do multiple things, do them well. Prove to others by your work that you can do the job, and you will be asked repeatedly to do a job.  Even with his limited formal education, he could do a job and do it well. He was a genius storyteller and could have everyone one in a room spellbound and laughing continuously in his presence.  You can do anything you put your mind to do.

My mother's father, Isham Spencer, Sr. worked 2 full-time jobs for years at a factory on 3rd shift, and then he came in and was the bus driver in the morning.  He did that for 20 plus years.  My mother and her family lived on a farm in the country, but they had to go to school for blacks only in the city.  Someone had to drive them there and why not their own father?  When my grandfather had to work over at the factory, my grandmother was his substitute driver.  My mother had 8 siblings, and that was one way that my grandfather could spend more time with his children.  And with 9 children, make extra money.  Where there is a will, there is a way.  Where there is eagerness, energy and expertise to perform well, I guarantee that there will an availability and opportunity.

So, as you can see, work is in my blood.  Now my father was the next generation, and he took the work ethic, multiple gifts and abilities to the next level. My dad worked full time as a teacher in the day and owned a cleaning service at night. At the height of his business, he had more than 50 employees. My mother ran that business for him in the daytime. She took care of everything so that he could teach kids, do lessons plans, receive two Masters degrees, two Ph.D.'s, be the Director of Christian Education and Deacon at our church as well as travel the world teaching others how to have a successful Christian Education department in their church. It's in my blood. I can't help it. I told my husband that working one job is not in my nature. I will use all of my gifts to generate income, benefit other people and fulfill my purpose. It's in my blood, and I can't help it. I could deny who I am and not carry on the legacy of my family, but who does that? I can't do that! Because the drive to succeed gets me up early in the morning, and keeps me up at night sometimes. I am an early riser, so I get ideas in my sleep. I get ideas in the shower, on the way to my teaching job and on the way back home to my house. I am God inspired, driven and motivated to be all that I can be while I am alive. As the old folks used to say, "Above ground."

What's down in you? What motivates you to go forward? Is it bills? Is it your family? Is it your legacy? Is it a dream, goal, vision, destiny and purpose? Whatever that it is, it needs to be ever present in your mind. Why? Because it will need to be the driving force to keep you going during the highs and lows of business.

Julia A. Royston

# Reflection: Is Business in Your Blood?

_____
_____
_____
_____
_____
_____
_____
_____
_____
_____
_____
_____
_____
_____
_____
_____
_____
_____
_____
_____

## It Starts with You

Even though I have all of this family history of this strong work ethic and multiple gifts in motion, I didn't have to follow suit and become an entrepreneur. Just because I can do multiple things didn't mean that I would actually do them. There are people out there who have many gifts, talents, abilities, skills and knowledge, and they never share it or make money doing it. I could have done the same. It's highly respectable to work one job, go home, go to church or on vacation and that be enough. To me, that is not enough. There is something down on the inside of me that says, "I can do, want and have more." I can hear and see ideas so clearly when I am asleep and awake. At times, these multiple gifts are in operation simultaneously and income generating. When one gift isn't generating revenue, another one is. Heritage, legacy and your family history might not be enough to motivate you. For your life to move forward in any direction, you have to buy in. You have to perform at your full capacity. You and I have to sharpen those skills to make sure that they are up to standard to get the best-desired results. It starts with me. Nobody can make me do it. I can shut down my business tomorrow if I wanted to, but I won't. I have clients who are depending on me, but I could choose to let them down too. It's called being selfish and irresponsible. I choose to be credible, responsible, full of integrity and do my best. Not perfect, but do my best. I choose to wake up every morning and work on positioning myself, my books and my business to be the most profitable. It starts with me. I agree that there are some things that are beyond my control, but how I behave, perform and produce is on me. It starts with me. I have an obsessive work ethic, but I also have ethics in my work.

It all starts with you too. You are the visionary, leader and determiner of your destiny. It is left up to you to decide first, what you want for yourself. What is the vision for your life? How do you want to live? How do you want your family to live? What quality of life, schedule and environment do you want to bring a business into? What type of business do you want to expose your family, friends and potential co-workers or employees to? You may ask, 'What does this have to do with turning your book into a business?' Everything. There will be distractions, life changes, people who do not want you to succeed with your book or your business, and you have to make it up in your mind what you want. I can't do it for you. I can't make you want something that you don't want. I can guide, direct and help you get there, but I can't make you want it. I will not be able to be there with you in the middle of every night to make that decision. Sure we can schedule a coaching call to focus your book and your business, but there are times that I won't be available for one reason or another. You've got to make it up in your mind that if nobody helps you, you will help yourself. If nobody believes in your book or business, you believe in it yourself. If none of your friends or family buys your book, sell it to a stranger. If nobody wants to pay you to speak about your book or business, be willing to go live on social media anyway to convince the world how much they need you and your book. How bad do you want it? That's a question for me to ask and only you can answer. So again I say, it starts with you. If you say yes that you would love for your book to turn into a business and you believe in it wholeheartedly, then we are ready for the next step.

## Drive, Determination and a Destination

Down inside of you must be the Drive, Determination and ultimately the inner vision of your successful Destination. You can't rely on others to always push you, pull you or direct you in a direction towards a destiny that others see that you don't see for yourself. You must have the ability to see that destination for yourself. So what do you see for you, your book and ultimately, your business? I don't know if it is the creativity down inside of me or what, but often I can see a book's potential more than the author can. Sure, that is a part of a publisher's job, but not all of the publisher's job. What if the publisher doesn't see your vision? Will you give up on your dream, goal and destiny for your book, because someone doesn't believe in it? Yes or No? I've seen people do it, but not me. I realize that if no one believes in it, I've got to believe in it. How badly do I want my vision to come to past? Very bad. I eat, sleep, drink and even up wide awake thinking about what kind of life I want for myself, my family and my business.

You have to be determined to get there through disappointment, discouragement and denials. People will deny you access to certain information, entries into specialized industries as well as resources to move to the next level. What do you do then? Go around them and find another route in. Just like the four friends in the Bible who wanted to get help for their friend that was lame. They couldn't go through the front door, side window or back door. If you are not familiar with the story, the four friends carried their friend on his bed onto the rooftop, tore off the roof and let their friend down through the ceiling to get him some help from Jesus. How determined are you to get the help for your book or business? If you need help from the bank, organization, coach or business to succeed, are you willing to go to extreme measures to get it done?  You reading this book tells me that you are willing to put in some effort to move your book to a business.  What will happen when a real obstacle comes along?  You will ask for help.  You will pick up a phone and try to get some information to solve your problem and meet that need.  I realize that you may ask, 'What does this have to do with your book becoming a business?  Everything.  Being in business takes effort.  Being in business is one of the hardest things that you will ever do.  Being in a successful business is the most rewarding thing that can ever happen to you.  Why?  Because you did it on your own.  Why?  Because it is something that you made happen for your business, family and life.  It feels different when you do something well for your own company with your name or brand on it than another company that categorizes you as an employee.

The route, networks, people, resources and information that it will take for your book and business to go to new or expanded levels and growth will be different. As someone who has written more than 40 books, each book has an individual place in the literary world. Each book went through a similar publishing process to come to life, but the results were different for each book. Why? My audience, subject of the book, book release and strategy for release may have been different and thus results varied. On the other hand, the determination to finish, the target audience and the message of the book, were in the forefront of my mind to make sure that the book was delivered in excellence. I had a vision for what I wanted the book to look like and be about.

For your future book, Determine in your mind and on paper what that looks like. Authors come to me and tell me that they have a message that can reach the world and should be for the world to see, but what world is that? Who are those people? What is it about your book that they would want to read? What inside of your book would impact or transform their lives? What should or could that transformation appear to be? Now, I know that you can't answer all of these questions because maybe the book has or has not been written. But throughout this process, that should be something on your mind. How will my book transform lives? Next, how can I make money from this transformation process or what type of business will I start? When you write a book that meets the needs of people or solves their problems, you will have no problem selling it. Additionally, people will come back to you over and over again to get more information from you or to do more business with you. Again, where are you taking your audience with your book and business? Are you wanting to transform their lives by coaching, products, services, conferences, masterminds or other ways to have long-term impact on their lives?

# Mind, Body and Soul

## What are You Thinking?

"Whatever the mind can conceive and believe, it can achieve." – Napoleon Hill

It all starts in the mind. Whatever you see in your head, can be accomplished on paper and through your actions. I have never known anyone who didn't get an idea that first came to them in their head. It may have derived from something that they saw on the street or watched on a television show, a book they read or a dream they had, but something was embedded in their mind from that encounter.

From that one encounter, if the idea is related to your passion, desires, gift, talent or ability, it won't let you rest until you do something about it. An idea that poignant won't let you rest until you do a simple Google search, watch a video about it, visit a library or ask an expert, but it will cause you to take some action. Even if the action renders a negative result, you must act.

People who say that they really have a desire to do something, be somewhere or have something, but they never move in the direction of that goal, it was only a fantasy. Anything that you really put your mind to do will cause your body to put an action behind your thoughts, desires and goals no matter how hard it gets. When you want it, you find a way.

Your mind is a powerful part of your anatomy. Mind over matter is true. You can will your body to do things that other people said that you couldn't do. Having the right mindset is as important as anything else you will do in making your book a business.

The right mindset will override anything else that attempts to block, stop or delay you from reaching any goal in life including making your book a business. Before we go any further, again I say, "It starts with you."

Even with the right mindset, you have to continually feed, renew or refresh your mind with the right thinking throughout the remainder of the process. You must keep your mind focused on that goal, vision and dream that you just said yes to. Why? Because everything and people around you will tell you not do it, it won't work or you will fail. Count on the critics to come. I look for them when I start something new. Sometimes the critics are those closest to you. When I hear the doubt, questions or concern in my mind, it is a good sign that I am embarking on something much bigger than where I am now. I am about to take on something so big that it will take God, my family, my team, every resource I have and every ounce of will and strength I embody to complete it.

You have to make it up in your own mind that you will do it, and you can do it. My father used to tell me, "If human beings can do it, you can too." I hear his voice inside my head and down in my heart each time I endeavor to do anything including writing this book. I not only tell myself I can do it, but I put into action what I want to do.

## What Do You See?

The body is an incredible thing but the brain is the central intelligence operation for the body. The brain, eyes, nose, mouth and ears are all located on the head. The head is the headquarters for the entire body. We could write an entire book on just what is going on inside the head. Beside your mindset, let's talk about how well you see. My eyesight is terrible. I started wearing glasses at age eight years old with vision numbers of 200/200. Normal eyesight is 20/20. My physical eyes were ten times worse than normal. Even though my physical need corrective lenses, my internal eyes are perfect. I see where I would love to go and strive daily to get there. I use that vision that is in my head and heart to drive me to invest in my business, continue to write what my audience wants to read and will buy. I encourage my authors even prior to the rough draft being finished to get a vision for your book. In week 5 of the 10-week writing course, we go on a writer's virtual field trip. We visit Amazon.com or any of the other online book distribution sites to get a look at the best seller, popular or higher selling books in their particular genre. We not only look at the cover design but the author bios, book descriptions and category descriptions. Your book is a business, so you need to get a vision for your book. How many books do you believe that you can sell? Who do you believe wants or needs to buy your book? Who do you want to serve with your book? We will talk about creating products and services surrounding your book much later, but right now concentrate on the book, the topic that you have written about and how it will impact someone else's life. Focus on the benefits of your book. Focus on the problem that your book will solve, as well as the pain that your book will ease for someone once your book is finished and purchased. Keep those people in your mind's eye, so that you will be on target your book's marketing, promotion and positioning in places that these particular people hang out virtually, as well as attend certain live events.

## What do you hear?

Your head has two things located on each side and those are your two ears. In my opinion, your ears are what will feed your brain more than what your mouth feeds the body. Why? What you hear is what you think about. What you think about is what you will eventually make a decision about. Ultimately, your choices will determine your actions. Be careful what you listen to. Be careful who you listen to. If you feed your ears negativity, you won't succeed. Feed your ears positive options from credible wise counsel. In the end, those words that you allowed in your ears will have an impact on you, so be careful. It's amazing how what I hear during the day, I can hear at night when I am sleeping. My unconscious mind is not asleep. That's the reason why if your loved one is in a coma and doesn't respond, the medical professionals still tell you to talk to the patient and tell them how much you love, care and miss them. They can hear you. The ears are transporting that love, care, hope, faith and positive energy to the brain in hopes that the person wakes up. So wake up that entrepreneur in you. Listen to good, sound and positive videos, audios and persons who want what's best for you, your business and your future.

## What Are You Saying?

There is power in your words. In addition to your ears being a source of nourishment, the words that you say out of your own mouth are a source of power. I remember when my business was first beginning. I invested a lot in the business, but it wasn't as profitable as my investment. There were several reasons why and those reasons have totally changed now, but my point is that first, I kept moving. Secondly, I told myself, I am going to be successful at this. Then, I told the naysayers, "We shall see." I didn't say what I was going to do exactly. But the old saying goes, "I can show you better than I tell you." I kept that phrase resonating in my head daily. Honestly, it is more important what you say to yourself than what you say to others. I had a graphic picture social media post that was reposted often, "Self-Talk: What are you saying to yourself?" What you say to yourself will fuel, drive, energize and motivate every action that you take. What you say to yourself will determine the next steps phone call that you make, the next partnership or alliance or that next move that you make to grow or expand your business. Be careful what you say to yourself. More importantly, be highly selective at what you say to others. Just "show them." Let your actions, results and success be greater than your conversation.

## You Are an Expert

One more thing to keep in mind with what you say is say to yourself, "I'm an expert." Yes, you are an expert. Say it until you believe it. Repeat the phrase, "I am an Expert" over and over to yourself no matter how strange it may sound to your ears. Why? Because when you write a book on any subject, you suddenly let the world know that you are an expert in some area or field of study. No matter what the subject is about. No matter if you learned it on a job or through an MLM company, or you saw someone else do it. You've learned something. You can do it well. There is a demand for that expertise from others, so walk in your expertise. Keep up with your field of study. Know who the other authors are in your field of study. Be able to know the magazines, blogs and websites that are trending in your subject area. The publishing, literary and writing industry came to me when one person asked me to publish their book. I had two options to give them. I could have said, 'yes or no.' Now, after saying yes to that one person when I could have said no, I now choose to say, "yes" multiple times over. Each time I publish a book, I also say yes to growing, changing, learning and improving to get better and better with each book. Looking at that first book that I published of someone else's I am still proud of it. But nine years later, I want to go back and make a lot of changes because I know more now. I know a lot more about the process of publishing books because I have more experience, see multiple points of view in the industry from the view of an author, librarian, publisher and business owner. The industry chose me, but I chose it right back. I am 'all in' in the book world. My life has completely changed because I have immersed myself in the literary industry. I teach, speak, publish and blog about writing. I coach writers. I also learn from other writers about writing. Ask my husband about all of the books that are in our house. Books have taken over parts of our house. Why? Because I am intricately a part of this business and this business is a part of me. After more than 9 years of publishing, 10 years of writing, more than 23 years as a certified librarian, 60+ signed authors to 2 publishing companies at this book publishing and 120+ books published, I can officially say that I have experience and knowledge about this industry. Do I know everything? Of course not. I must continue to learn, keep up with trends on a daily basis to be a leader in my field of study. You are an expert because you have an expertise in a subject area. Expert is not synonymous with perfection, but it means that you possess a level of expertise on a topic that others don't have. You know things that others don't know or even want to know. People want to pay you for what you know. Accept your expertise status embrace it. On the other hand, always keep learning, refining and discovering more and more about your field of study. Even after my dad retired from being a teacher for 29 years, he kept up with the field. He read books, articles in magazines, watched any documentary on educational trends and features on educators. Why? This was his life. Make sure that the book topic that you are writing about is in your heart, mind and life. Be willing to give yourself to it, and I promise it will give back to you.

## Do people want the book that you are writing?

This is the hardest question that I have for authors. As a writer, I love a great story. As a publisher, I want to know what the people want, what books will people be moved to buy and then tell others about. Are people actually buying or even want the book that is down in your heart to write? Are you, the author even connected to people that have an interest in the expertise or subject area that you are writing about? You love it, but will other people love it enough to buy it? How do you know? Ask. Do your homework and do some research on the bestselling books out there right now. I can tell at the events I go to what people are standing in line to buy. Sure the author may be a famous celebrity and that may be a large part why people are buying the book. On the other hand, what is the book about? A self-help book about how to do better in life? How to make more money? Romance fiction?

## Reflection

What book is inside of you? What are you passionate about?

_____
_____
_____
_____
_____
_____
_____
_____
_____
_____
_____
_____
_____
_____
_____

# The Book

If you are reading this, you have said yes to this process. You want it. Sometimes we have said yes to things that we fully don't know what we are getting involved in until we said yes. Trust me, I know. I didn't know what was all involved in the business that I said yes to, but it is mine, I love it and there is no turning back. It will not all be easy and sometimes you will feel like quitting, but there will be rewards along the way that will keep you going. So let's talk about your book.

**Tell me about your book**

That is the first phrase that I ask authors who reach out to me about publishing their book. "Tell me about your book." When I make that statement, I am waiting to hear it in your voice.

If I'm meeting you in person or via video conferencing, see on your face your connection to the book. I want to see and hear your passion about the topic and its contents. In that first meeting, if you can't convince me that you really are tied to the topic in that first meeting, then I have more work to do than producing a book to sell. I can do that in my sleep, but what I can't produce is a passion, burning desire and an 'eat, sleep and drink' connection to the book's topic. I am being honest as a publisher. Your connection to your topic tells me how productive you are going to be as an author. As a business owner, it tells me how well your book is going to sell. As an author, it tells me how much you know about the topic. You don't have to know how to write the book to tell me about the topic. I should hear it in your voice and see it on your face. I often use the example of a new grandmother with a new grandchild and how her face lights up, her voice changes pitch and the phone is immediately unlocked to show you pictures or video. The love is evident, and the sometimes the tears even flow about this love of her life. Your book is your new baby. Your book should be the new love of your life. Your book should light up your face and change the pitch of your voice to immediate excitement, enthusiasm and energy. The phrase, "I can't wait to tell you about my book," should be on the tip of your tongue, and no one even asked. Make sure that you are passionate about the topic of your book.

## Reflection: Tell me about your book.

## The Topic or Subject of Your Book is Your Business

This book is focusing on your book, turning into a business. Writing a book that will eventually be a business requires more passion, energy and focus, than even writing a book that you enjoy or take pleasure in sharing. The topic that you will write about in the book that I am encouraging you to write will be your business. If you are writing about domestic violence, faith, money, business or empowerment issues, you are now in that business and offering that service. You will now be considered an expert in that subject area and you will be a lifelong student of that topic.

Make sure that if you don't know much about it, that you will sit down and become an avid research and student of that topic. When I published my first book, I did my best and it was successful. When I published the first book of someone else's, I was panicking because someone was paying me to do it. I did my homework, I asked questions, I had others help me and was still nervous at the book signing that something wasn't right. I am more comfortable now after more than nine years, but still a student and learning my craft. The book that will be transformed into a business is now 'your baby.' This book will be consuming your thoughts, ideas and plans. You will be networking and introducing your baby to everyone you meet. You will have inventory of your baby everywhere you go. We will convey and help you discover new ways and profitable avenues to introduce your topic and book business to the world.

**Reflection:** Based on the topic, what do you want to teach? How do you want to impact people's lives with your book?

_____
_____
_____
_____
_____
_____
_____
_____
_____
_____
_____
_____
_____
_____
_____
_____
_____
_____
_____
_____

## Vision for Your Book

At this point, I usually ask an author what you are passionate about. I used to say that, 'Whatever you are passionate about will sell," but now I am not so sure. You have to make sure that your passion, business, product or service, is what the people want to buy it before you take the time and spend the money to write the book. You may love a subject, topic or genre of book, but if people are not buying it, should you spend the time writing it and make it into your business? Probably not. But, I will say this, 'If it is a book with a topic that can help someone save time, money or make more money or solve a great problem, it will sell.

**Reflection:** Where do you see your book going? To just your family and friends or around the world? How much effort are you willing to put in to making that vision come to past?

_____
_____
_____
_____
_____
_____
_____
_____
_____
_____
_____
_____
_____
_____
_____
_____
_____
_____
_____
_____

## The Cover is the Face

My publishing company is designed to work along with the author and be a partnership with the author.  Once you explain the topic of your book and I am about to feel your passion for your book, we map out a strategy along with a vision for your book.  What the book should look like is the next phase of producing a high-quality product that people will want to buy and share.  I realize that a personal connection with your book is necessary and the vision that you have for your book is crucial.  One thing that I strive to convince authors of is, that the cover of the book has to make sense, be attractive and eye-catching enough for the reader to open, review and buy the book.  Some authors will not budge from the cover that they had in mind; and at times, they are totally correct in their vision.  It goes along exactly with what is inside the book and along with their business branding that we will talk about later. Other times, the vision for the cover does not coincide with the book's topic or contents at all. The book cover is the face of the book. We need to make the face of the book as attractive as possible. This book's cover can be changed later if necessary, but we don't want the book's cover to have to change if we get it right the first time. Follow the guidance of an experienced publisher in this area. If you don't agree with the publisher, ask your readers or potential audience to look at the cover and see if the cover is representative of what you said the book is about. Believe you me, people will tell you the truth. I have had enough authors display their cover options on social media and people love giving their opinion no matter the author's feelings. I tried to explain to an author once that their people on the cover probably wasn't the best idea, but they wanted it in spite of my suggestion. I asked them to put it to their audience, and the audience agreed with me. The author agreed with her audience and has done extremely well with her book. If your book hasn't sold well, ask someone to tell you the truth about the cover. Don't ask your parents, because they love everything you do. Unless you have a mother like mine who will tell you the truth and hold nothing back. I digress, but ask someone do they like the cover? Be ready to accept the truth for the benefit of your book and your business. Not only accept the truth but change the cover. I admit that I changed the cover on my book, "Everyday Miracles" and it totally changed everything about the reception and sales of the book.

**Reflection:** What does your book look like? Have you seen other books like what you have in mind?

_____
_____
_____
_____
_____
_____
_____
_____
_____
_____
_____
_____
_____
_____
_____
_____
_____
_____
_____
_____

## Content is King

The cover gets them to open the book, but the content inside will keep your reader reading the book and connecting with you; the author. If you provide quality content and information that a reader can use in their business, organization or life, they will want to know more about you. They hopefully will turn into a follower, fan and loyal supporter of other things that you do. My goal with this book is for you to get the information you need to turn your book into a business, to help you become a productive leader in your topic and more importantly, be profitable. The message or topic of your book should be credible, concise and clear enough for the reader to take the information and put it into action. You can't tell everything in a book. You have to get the basic concepts down, action steps and provide resources or products for the reader to progress to productivity. There is only so much information that a person can retain, given that the attention span of people is very short in this technological age. So if your book is a non-fiction, self-help book, jump right into the '7 ways to do whatever.' Don't spend a lot of time with too much background information that is not intricately related to the topic. Give them the 'meat and potatoes' in chronological or step by step order. If the ideas that you are presenting are not all yours, give credit and cite your source of where the ideas originated. Plagiarism is real, and lawyers love to sue. Protect yourself and your content, but also be mindful and give credit to the ideas of others.

The ultimate goal is for your book to be a foundational tool that your business is built upon.

If you need basic help writing a book, obtain the book, "Write that Book Now" at http://bit.ly/writethatbooknow

**Develop sub-topics or themes related to your book**

What are some subtopics or sub-themes of your book?  If the book is about beauty, what aspect of beauty?  Self-image, hair, make-up, skincare, inner or emotional beauty?  Realize that a book can be expanded and extended into multiple areas related to the topic of your book especially non-fiction books.  In my industry, there are multiple facets to publishing and not just producing a book to sell.  Publishing and successful publishing is related to sales, distribution, marketing, promotion and the audience of the book.

**Reflection:** List some sub-topics for your book

_____
_____
_____
_____
_____
_____
_____
_____
_____
_____
_____
_____
_____
_____
_____
_____
_____
_____
_____
_____

## Products and Services

How are you going to make money without any products or services? I don't know so let's talk about some products, services or ways to generating money.

To have products and services to sell, you will have to create additional products and services which can be many and change over time, and definitely not all be included in this book right here. For our time together, I am going to focus on a few crucial products and services to help turn your book into a profitable business. Yes, if you have a book, you are in the book business. If you have a business, you need a book. Let's talk about a few products. I offer product creation classes to create all of these products together in a group coaching session.

Let's talk about creating some products and services for your book. Visit http://bit.ly/talkwithroyston and schedule a time to talk with me about how we can create additional products, services and profits for your book.

**Book**

I am in the book business, so I am going to start with the first 3 products related and relevant to your business is a book. As I stated before, every business needs a book. If you have not written a book, I encourage you to do so. Why? First, a book is your voice to the world. It puts in printed form what you want to say related to your business, expertise and legacy even after you have departed this life. Secondly, your book can be platform building, branding identity and industry credibility. What that means, in a nutshell, is that a book connected and related to your business can set you apart, and help you to stand out in your particular field or industry.

If you would like to know more about creating, publishing and promote your book, visit http://bit.ly/writethatbooknow or http://bit.ly/writepublishpromoteitnow.

**EBook**

In my opinion, I do not believe that eBooks will totally replace paperback books. But consider this, the ability to have a book on your computer, laptop, tablet and phone as well as a paperback to read on the beach is vastly growing as a preferred means of reading a book and gathering information. Presently, all of my packages with my publishing company deliver the finished manuscript in paper and electronic format. It is now standard and not an option. I believe that the more media formats that your message is available, there should be more opportunities for a larger audience.

EBooks can also be used in your business in multiple ways. You can sell them on your website, along with a class, workshop or conference or simply produce something short enough to be a lead magnet or give a way. If you are new or establishing your credibility in your industry area, people are more likely to get a free download in exchange for their email address rather than purchasing the eBook from you.

For more information on creating eBooks for your business, visit http://bit.ly/roystonebooks.

**Audiobook**

Some people do not really like to read a book for themselves in paperback, hardback or eBook format, but want the book read to them. Audiobooks do that. You can put on your headphones and do your workout. Some people put their Audiobook in the audio jack of the car and drive for hours listening to an audiobook. It is a separate stream of income, market, formatting and audience that loves and will pay for audiobooks.

Audiobooks can be recorded by the author or you can contract others to record your books. I have recorded in a recording studio, but there are some high-quality recording devices that you can do in the privacy of your own home.

Don't wait. Record it yourself or pay someone to record it for you, and don't miss out on money or the responses from those who will love your story in audio format.

**Class/Courses/Workshops**

What do you know how to do? Whatever that thing, subject, project or skill is to teach it! A workshop is a great way to display what you know to a larger group instead of one on one. The things to primarily consider is if your audience is willing to attend a live face to face event or a virtual event online from the comfort of their home. Remember that you should charge for the workshop as well. If it important to people they should be willing to pay for the workshop. People will also engage and appreciate you and your content more if you charge for the information. You can add a journal, a pen and peppermint for live event, but charge. If you are having a virtual event, charge for it as well, but offer a glam bag or goodie bag to add more value to your virtual event.

If you need help developing a workshop, reach out to us at julia@bkroystonpublishing.com or visit www.bkroystonpublishing.com or schedule a time at http://bit.ly/talkwithroyston.

**Videos**

Videos clearly fulfill the saying, 'a picture is worth a thousand words' to the 10th degree. Today, that same picture now has animation, sound, other images, text and music added to make the picture even more appealing and interactive. A video grabs the viewer's attention. A link added to that same video at the beginning, middle and end can add money to the pockets of the producer of the video. Videos should be authentic and don't have to be polished to be effective. We have seen the horrible videos of murders spark protests and riots in the streets across this country. We have seen dancers, singers and other artists display their talents and land multi-million dollar contracts and become world famous. We have seen educators, coaches and trainers provide video courses, and become famous, profitable and transform lives around the world from their videos. Memories are made, savored and cherished through video. The video commentary surrounding the message of your book should be the introduction to your website, course or program. There are so many ways that video can be used with your book, business and product line that it is a crucial and critical piece of the business equation. It is no longer an option, but a necessity. Whether you utilize a several hundred dollar HD camera or your phone, make it meaningful, content-rich and come straight from the heart and watch how it will reach the masses.

**Live Streaming**

Live Streaming is a phenomenon that has turned everyday people into superstars. Now, you may say, that is Youtubers. Maybe. But there are everyday people that have accessed Periscope, Facebook LIVE, Instagram LIVE, and stream live through YouTube that are making money. Live Streaming allows you to go LIVE and access people around the world; especially Periscope, and introduce yourself, your message and your products and services. I have gained clients, developed a following and advanced my business significantly through live streaming. Another benefit is that these same live stream videos and events can be saved, uploaded to a YouTube Channel or your own platform/website, and the content can be resold, saved and re-promoted on another platform and new audience. How cool is that?! Now, you may be hesitant, nervous or apprehensive about going live, because you don't know what to say, want to be perfect or self-conscious of how you look and sound. Don't be! Push the live button and go for it. There are billions of people on the planet. Someone will connect, follow and like what you have to say and how you say it. Talk about your business and what you have to offer someone. Talk about your dog. Talk about how beautiful the day is that day. Talk about something that will encourage someone. There will be people who want to buy what you have to sell. There will be people who will share with others what you have to sell. There will be people who will never buy what you have to sell, but don't stop. Push the live button and talk to the world through Live Streaming!

**Webinars**

Webinars are defined as 'a seminar conducted over the Internet.' This is a general definition, but what is the purpose of the seminar and what do you want the person to do once they have left your webinar? We now know that a Webinar should do several things when concluded. First, you should have the end result in mind. What do you want to say? Who do you want to reach? After you have them attracted, what do you want them to do? How will it be done; click a link, call a number or submit an email? Secondly, during the webinar session, it should inform your audience, reader or prospective client about a new service, product or opportunity that should be beneficial and they have an interest. There should be a way for the people to ask questions and a landing page or link should be provided. Finally, it should require that the person provide an email address or have opportunity to submit their email address in exchange for free information that is related to the webinar topic or service. Their permission and submission of their email address will provide a way for you to connect, correspond and collaborate with the receiver in a way that will have them interested in what you have to say a product or service in the future or attend another virtual or in-person event in the future. For more information on webinars, how to create them and what tools are needed, there is a class available titled, 'Product Creation 2: Audiobooks, Workbooks and Webinars' available at http://bit.ly/roystonproducts2.

**Live Events/Conferences/Retreats**

For more than 30 years of my life, I have hosted and attended conferences. I used to be a youth conference coordinator at my home church when I was a teenager. As an adult, I have hosted my own retreats, workshops and conference virtually and in-person. The key to a successful conference is the topic, the location, the people and marketing not to mention, the price of admission and when it will be held.

The topic of the conference should be relevant, exciting and wanted. There is nothing worse than having a conference about something that no one is interested in anymore. How about the topic, "The Benefits of VHS Videos?" Would you be interested in attending a conference on that topic? You can host it and market it, but I can almost guarantee that no one will come. Why? We don't use VHS videos anymore. Ask Blockbuster. I digress. Now you could turn that around and have a tech conference about trends in technology since VHS videos, and people may show up.

The location of the conference is just as crucial as the topic, speakers and marketing. The topic, the audience and marketing may be on point, but some people won't attend because of the location. Not enough parking, the food is terrible, it's usually crowded and the bathrooms are small; just to name a few. I will be transparent and tell you that I thought an author retreat would be great in a hotel, but not my audience. They wanted a retreat center in the woods somewhere instead of a plush hotel. Location, location, location should be strongly considered prior to hosting a conference.

Pricing must be set just right for the area of the country, type of event and the audience that you wish to attract. You must also consider the social-economic level of the audience that you do attract rather than who you want to attract. As with any relationship, you have to build the relationship in order for them to come.

You can't be hanging out with and serving $10 admission people and put a price tag of $999 as a registration fee. Did you ask your audience would they be willing to come to a conference that you were hosting and pay $999? That question would be at the forefront of my mind. Now, if I had hosted a sold-out conference at $15 a person and wanted to raise it to $20 per person, there might not be too much resistance. Try raising the price to $150, and see how much your Eventbrite is ringing.

Marketing and promotion is another key to hosting a conference. If no one knows about it or you don't tell the right people or people who would be interested about the conference, then you should not move forward with the idea of conference. Conferences are work but can be worth it if you surround yourself with a team that can help push, promote and propel your event to the next level.

Hosting a conference is a way to dig deeper and actually break down into manageable pieces or workshops the message of your book or business. It is also a way to partner and collaborate with other speakers, coaches and authors surrounding the same topic. In the collaborative effort, you should make sure that these partners market the event to their audiences as well pitch their books, products and services. I usually see more pitching for profits going on than marketing and promoting the event by each and every speaker or presenter. A speaker contract may have to be created and if the terms of the agreement are not adhered to, that speaker should not return to speak on your platform. Just a thought.

In addition to the subject matter being discussed; if you obtain sponsors, vendors or other donors, it can be a profitable venture for you, the sponsors to be mentioned at the event as well as you providing services for those in attendance.

I spend more time with conferences because it takes time, money and effort to host a profitable, informative and successful conference. Multiple aspects must be considered prior to hosting your first or any future conference.

If you need assistance or advice regarding planning a conference or would like for me to speak at your next conference, don't hesitate to reach out to us at julia@bkroystonpublishing.com or schedule an appointment at http://bit.ly/talkwithroyston.

**Retreats**

I love retreats. I don't go on as many retreats as I would like. I was introduced to retreats when I was a private Catholic school librarian and teacher and was a teacher leader at a retreat. I can get so much more done without distractions at retreats. Now, I conduct retreats for authors and business owners, because I want to help them get work done but it is also income generating for me and my company. A retreat should be thought out to include as much time for planning, action and reflection. There should be instruction, but don't pack the schedule too full that there is not time enough for networking, collaboration or coaching.

If you need assistance or advice regarding planning a retreat or would like for me to speak at your next retreat, don't hesitate to reach out to us at julia@bkroystonpublishing.com or schedule an appointment at http://bit.ly/talkwithroyston.

**Intensives**

Have you ever attended a class or workshop, and there were more questions, information to dispense or opportunity to dig deeper into the topic but you ran out of time? Have you ever had a class where you had all levels in the class and it seemed that the entry level people's questions were always answered? Because of the time, it left little time for those with advanced knowledge of the topic to get their needs addressed?  This is just two scenarios or questions that arise and give need to create an intensive workshop. An intensive is more thorough or in my estimation, an advanced course.  I wouldn't suggest a beginner take an intensive course unless you intend to cover the basics and advanced aspects of the course in one intensive course.  The information that will be covered in the intensive course should be thoroughly explained so that those that sign up for the course will know exactly what they will be learning.  If prerequisites are required, give details of what they need to know before they take this course or if there is a course that you offer that has the prerequisites that they need. Intensives are a great way to take the topic, the attendees and the knowledge learned more deeply and expand the level of thought to a much high level.

For more information or help with any of the topics covered, reach out to us at http://bit.ly/talkwithroyston, and we will be happy to discuss it further and offer you opportunities for creating these products for your own book and business.

## Reflection: What Product or Service will You Create?

_____
_____
_____
_____
_____
_____
_____
_____
_____
_____
_____
_____
_____
_____
_____
_____
_____
_____
_____
_____
_____
_____
_____

# Systems

I am a solopreneur by nature. I recently realized that to truly take my business to the next level, I will need people and systems in place and running smoothly to make that happen. Before we get to the people, we need to determine the systems that we will need for this book and business. Once the systems are in place, we can plug in the people to help move and further those systems to even more impactful and profitable.

## Be Legal

I must be honest and tell you that I have control issues. I desire to own, steer and control all aspects of my book and business. Having that ownership requires that I have legal ownership of my intellectual property as well as filing my business with the Secretary of State in the state that I live in.

Intellectual Property is defined as "a work or invention that is the result of creativity, such as a manuscript or a design, to which one has rights and for which one may apply for a patent, copyright, trademark and etc."(www.dictionary.com) Therefore, anything that you have produced you should protect by law from anyone to steal, copy or take as theirs. For trademarks or patented materials, I suggest that you consult with a lawyer and specifically intellectual property attorneys who specialize in patents and trademarks. There is a lot of work that you can do ahead of time, and I advise you to do your homework. I have submitted copyright applications for my music as well as my and author's books. Visit www.copyright.gov for all of the information on getting your literary, sound, images, software or other items copyrighted. There is a complete list of the materials that can be copyrighted as well as what forms to use and the fees associated with being legal.

As far as your business filings and status, I suggest that you consult with a CPA, corporate attorney or other professional business or financial adviser about your status. Your status will determine your filing status, pay taxes and any other tax breaks or obligations required by your state. Know your state's laws and requirements for each filing status before making that decision. An informed decision is the best. Make sure that you explore the negatives and positives of each status. Don't listen to anyone except a professional, certified and licensed consultant. It could cost you tremendously if you listen to the wrong person. Contact your particular state's Small Business Association, and ask them about the opportunities available for women, minorities and veterans. Based on the subject of your book and the industry category of your business, it will determine how your business will or may be classified for tax and corporate filing status.

## **Marketing and Promotion Systems**

With regards to marketing and promotional strategies, I must confess that this area is a constant learning process for me. Marketing and promotions must be done, studied, learned and relearned with each new product, service and technology outlet that becomes available. I believe the biggest issue with regards to marketing and promotion, is who you know and how many people you know that are interested in the book's message and book business that you are building. I know so many great books that are written, but no one knows about them or wants to know about the book after it is written. Therefore, you must study marketing and promotional outlets for your book and business. What are the marketing and promotional avenues out there to be accessed?  Here is a short list:

Newspapers

Magazines

Radio (Traditional and Online)

Television

Videos

Audio

Podcasts

Advertisement (Paid, Free, Online and Print)

Social Media

Social Media Ads

Newsletters

Blogs (Your own or being a guest blogger)

## Books

I have written, "Promote that Book Now" to offer suggestions and avenues for promoting your book, go to http://bit.ly/writepublishpromoteitnow to get your eBook copy.

I have only written a book titled, "30 Ways to turn your words into wealth." These are ways to market, promote and expand the reach of your book and its message. To access and obtain the full list of 30, go to http://bit.ly/30waysformoney.

I am certain that there will be other promotional outlets invented in the future; but in the meantime, this book should get you started. As a bonus idea, I suggest that you keep up with the latest and greatest things that are sure to come out in the marketplace to take full advantage of these new outlets. Also, create a demand and generate an additional profitable stream of income in the book business.

## Sales System

There are a few areas in my life where I know I need help, and sales is one of them. I always congratulate myself when someone agrees to buy what I have to offer. Why? Because I am just myself. I don't have any real strategies to convince you to buy the book, enroll in the class or attend my live event. I just ask, show you why it would benefit you, explain what we will cover and put a buy button on it and hope you go for it. A real sales system is not that way. First, if you are a real salesperson, you can get any person to buy anything. You have the charisma, words to say, product benefits and can get generally discern about the person and get them to buy the product, plain and simple. In the words of a teacher friend of mine, "Girl, I can sell ice in Alaska." I believe she could do it too. My friend is a teacher and not quite ready for full-time sales. But if you have the money, you might convince her. On the other hand; if she says no and you still have the money, find an experienced salesperson to be on your team. It will save you time and effort to learn the sales strategies and tactics you need to close the deal. While you are looking at your budget, you can't let products hang out on your bookshelves. Like me, you've got to move them somehow. So first, let's agree seriously on something: Everyone is not going to buy your book. Everyone is not going to enroll in your class. Everyone is not going to help you move your book into a profitable business, but you can determine who wants the book that you have written. You can find out who has a question, need or pain that your book answers, fulfills the need and eases that specific pain. Find where these people hang out. Be willing to invest in yourself enough to go where these people hang out with inventory to sell to them.

On the other hand, you have to make sure that your product is worth them buying it at the price that you set. For example, there are people who have self-published their books; and it is a viable option, but, why would someone need or want a publisher? My prices are reasonable and comparable to other publishing companies out there, but some make the choice to hire a publisher because they don't want to do it themselves. They would prefer to pay someone to do it for them. I take that same premise to the next level and offer those who want to self-publish the opportunity to get my services, whatever service they need, pay for it and still self-publish. So I add value and variety for the customer to access my services. I avail my customers who want to publish a book the full range of services, options to participate and costs associated with each service ala carte or as a package. I made the adjustment in my business practices after receiving calls from people with these requests. I said yes to the flexibility, made a sale and gained a new customer. Finally, once you have met the right people and offered them the right product at the right price, make sure that all of your sales outlets can accept the payment that they have. Do your links work on your website? Do you have change if you are at a large event or festival? Do you have credit card capability? Can you provide an invoice, Purchase Order or W-9 if selling to librarians? Don't work so hard getting the sale that you are not able to complete the sale. If you need help, don't hesitate to reach out to http://bit.ly/talkwithroyston.

## Branding System

Most people think that when you start talking about branding, it is the logo, your colors, the website, business cards, posters and etc. After 9 ½ years in business, the most important thing is 'You.' You are the first part of the brand that is the most important. The essential is question I asked is, 'What do people get when they work with you?' Not just the results. What will the experience be like if people work with or go into a partnership with you? The logo, business cards, website and the most beautiful color scheme ever mean nothing, if you don't represent your brand correctly. Have you ever been to a store that had exactly what you needed, but the salesperson was so nasty that you left the store and went somewhere else? That's what you don't want to happen. Therefore, be clear about what you are offering and deliver on what you say you can deliver in excellence. Now, mistakes happen. Companies don't ship or deliver when they say they will due to major storms or catastrophes, but you should have more victories than losses. You should have more satisfied customers than dissatisfied customers. You should have more people referring you than not referring you. You should have more people wanting to work with you than telling people to stay away from you. You are the first key to your branding system. After you have laid the groundwork at the beginning of your business and book release with a great reputation based on your integrity, character, work and work ethic, then your logo, colors, postcards, business cards, banner and other accessories will be gladly received. I guarantee you that your audience will gladly help you select the logo and share it with their friends and others because they believe in you and know your work rather than the color and design of the logo.

## Payment Systems

I find that this is one of the biggest problems for authors and business owners, and that is how, where and when to get paid. You would think that this is a no-brainer, but it is not. We have to think of the customer and not what is convenient for us. Sure some people would like to accept cash only, but that is not realistic. We live in a cashless society. I was on a plane recently and for the non-complimentary alcoholic drinks, they didn't accept cash at all; only credit cards. I have seen authors lose sales because they didn't have a way to accept credit cards. Don't let this be you.

I utilize PayPal.com for most of my credit card payments. Open a PayPal.com account and with the business account you can send invoices, accept credit cards as well as receive money in amounts not invoiced for donations, etc. The major issue with PayPal is that they don't accept money in every single country. You would think that they would, but there are some countries that they don't do business with.

I have a Square account available at www.squareup.com that I use in conjunction with my phone to accept credit cards at large festivals, conferences and outside events.

I have a Merchant account that I use through my business account for credit card transactions of large amounts, countries that PayPal does not serve and for American Express or other cards, not Visa or MasterCard.

I also use the Cash app that allows for people to make cash payments directly from their bank account to my bank account. This works well for subcontractors to my business such as graphic designers, musicians or other artists/authors.

I do not want any person to be left out that wants to pay me for my books, music or other products or services. Establish a Payment system with one or more of these entities, so that you can get paid no matter if you are on the street, on your computer or on the phone.

## Email Marketing System

Email marketing is a way that you market your business, book, products and services to an audience that has voluntarily signed up for to be on your email list. Your purpose is to build relationships, establish trust, give important information and then see if the people on the list are interested in more information, other products, and services, attend a live event, conference, workshop or retreat. This is done simply through email. Of course, it depends on the message, the catchy phrases in the subject line as well as any other way through the power of persuasion through words to get them to buy or participate. In the beginning, I didn't have a clue that I was even conducting email marketing. I traveled and sang to more than 75 events a year for years. Once I produced my first CD project; when I met someone at an event, I asked them to write down their email address and on a monthly basis, I would send them a newsletter. My newsletter had encouragement, calendar of where I was going to be and link to where you could buy my CD and then later my books. People enjoyed the newsletters, but I didn't have any action buttons and/or links that people could click on directly and buy the product. They usually had to email me and order or go to Amazon and order and/or see me at the next event. I now use GetResponse.com email marketing system and when you click on the link, it takes you directly to PayPal where you can put your credit card information or log into your PayPal account and pay for the item, services or event. Some would say email is dead, I don't think so. I still get responses and people who purchase products and services via my email marketing system. The biggest problem is I have grown my list as much as I should. I am making up for that by creating ways for people to voluntarily get on my list including forms and hyperlinked images on my website. I do giveaways at large events that require your email address to participate. Now, I do not put you on my list automatically from this event. I send you a general email thank you for registering for the free offer, and then send you a link or make another offer with some other product. If you click on it and add yourself to my list, that is fine. Another benefit of the email marketing system is you get to see which emails that people open, what day and at what time they open the emails. With different email marketing systems, you can host webinars, create landing pages or sales pages as well as follow-up automatic emails to market to the people on your list. You may not be ready for an email marketing system; but no matter what system you use, make sure that you have a way to collect email address at each and every event you attend. You can have a giveaway to collect emails. You can have people text a specific number to obtain their email. Whatever way you choose, you have to have a way to connect and communicate with your audience. With that being said, let's talk more about communication systems.

**Communication/Follow-up System**

I recently reached out to an eBook distributor with a problem. They informed me that they only respond to support issues via email. No phone calls, text messages, instant messages or chat services were available. Send an email and wait. I couldn't believe it, and as a customer I was outraged. I was stuck. There was no way around it. I waited, got a response after 2 days, responded and we have been corresponding ever since. But know this, I am looking for alternatives instead of working with that organization. I don't want my only way to interact with you to be via email. I am the same way with my clients. I give you multiple ways to interact with me. I have people that don't care the time of day, night, morning, weekend or hour, they will reach out. I may not be available to respond right at that moment, but I will respond: Facebook Messenger, Instagram, Twitter, email, phone and/or text. It might be easier via text because I don't have to actually talk to you but can text while in a meeting, in my car (my husband is driving, lol) or folding clothes. I believe in office hours and putting limits on conversations during dinner or early hours. But if you are looking to grow an international, multi-time zone business or reach with your book, you are going to have to be more flexible and accessible.

Secondly, there needs to be a consistent communication system. Are you going to send out a newsletter monthly or quarterly? Will there be weekly or monthly emails that go out to your email list? Hopefully, your email marketing system will enable you to send out newsletters with templates provided that make it convenient to communicate with your audience. You should attempt a system that will have multi-capabilities rather than having to have multiple systems to meet the communication and email needs of your business.

Finally, after the email marketing and communication system, you need a system to keep up with potential clients, readers and leads for sales. Until I knew better, I used my calendar and just wrote it down. People that I met and said they were interested in writing a book, buying a book or liked a book, went into the calendar. This worked for a while when I only had a few clients and people didn't know that I wrote or published books. But as word spread and others found out about my publishing companies and even more people started referring me, I knew I had to have a better system. It doesn't mean that some people don't fall through the cracks; but overall, I am able to get and keep people in my email system and communicate with them. I use GetResponse, but I also have a Virtual Assistant who does initial calls and some return calls and helps me to keep track of the who, what, when and the where I met them and how they were connected to me. The Follow-up system is so critical to not only getting, but also keeping clients coming back to do business with and referring you to others. There are tons of websites out there that provide communication and follow-up systems or CRM (Customer Relationship Management) systems out there. Do your research? Ask others in the social media world what CRM or communication follow-up system that they use. This is critical for MLM businesses, so ask. A CRM system can save you time, customer and a business. What is your communication/follow-up system going to be?

## Delivery and Distribution System

I was a vendor at a writer's conference and there was another vendor that had beautifully handcrafted books but no ISBN, barcodes or distribution system. The books were beautiful and well done, but their publishing and delivery system was traditional at best. They received submissions from every other publisher. They produced the books, but you could order them on their website or they mailed them out to the authors, customers and bookstores that wanted to purchase them and sell them. Delivery for print books is the same for all of us. My publishing company would have the books printed and have them shipped to the address of your choice as well. You can order books through the publisher's website, from the author's website or the distributor's website. It looks the same until you realize that with a Delivery and Distribution system in place, you are able to have books delivered to your customer without you doing anything. The distributor makes sure that the customer has the printed book delivered to their house and takes care of payment, shipping, tax and handling cost collection for you. Now the distributor wants a distribution fee for doing this action, but this is where 'making money while you sleep' is in action. My publishing company receives notices from the distributor when a book has sold and royalty payments once a quarter. How will your book, products, services, courses, workshops and conferences be delivered to your customers? How will they gain access to your services with or without you? Will you need to be a part of every aspect of delivery and distribution or will you contract with a service to make sure that anywhere around the world at any time someone can gain access to what you are selling? It is a beautiful thing. Having an automated, on-demand systems in place has revolutionized the cable television, video and film industry. People want to view television shows, videos, films and other special events when they want to and not when a programming guide says that they have to. It's the same with your book, class, conference or other product. Give the customer a link, portal or email access when they pay and let the distribution, delivery and the success of utilizing the product, service or event begin when they want to and not when you tell them that they have to. I realize that this information can be overwhelming at times, but reach out to me at julia@bkroystonpublishing.com or visit http://bit.ly/talkwithroyston and let's discuss the many ways and get you the information to make that happen in your book business. Let's go!

**Reflection:** What Systems do you need for your book and business?

_____
_____
_____
_____
_____
_____
_____
_____
_____
_____
_____
_____
_____
_____
_____
_____
_____
_____
_____
_____

# The Dream Team

There are people in your life that will be there to cheer you on, love you no matter what and tell people that you are the best at everything. That's what we call family. We love family until the end. We don't get to pick our family members; whether they are good or bad. We just love them. In business, family can be good for us and sometimes family cannot be good for our business. Only you can determine how family will be involved and ultimately impact your business.

## Inner Circle

This is one of the biggest lessons that I have had to learn after starting my business. It is not that I don't like people, I am really a people person. It is not that I don't need help, but it is hard to accept the help that At first, I didn't feel like I could afford to pay anyone to help me; but when I could afford it, I still didn't have a team. After so many years, I realized that I wasn't able to plan, prepare or point the business in the right direction unless I had a team to do repetitive or learned tasks. I needed a team. I needed to figure out a way to build a team. I believe it has to do with being able to do multiple things. This is an asset and a liability. Why? I can't lead the work or be a visionary for the work because I spend so much time doing the work. So I had to figure out a few things. First, who I can teach to do the repetitive tasks that I no longer have time to do in my business? Secondly, who can I teach do the things that I do not do well at all? Finally, who do I trust that can perform well when I'm not looking, and I don't have to supervise them? The last issue is probably the hardest because being able to trust people in my place to speak for my business is so important to me. Why?

These people would be representing you, your brand and your business. I realize that they won't get it perfect all of the time, but you have to equip them, give them the parameters in which to work and then let them work.

Your inner circle should have your vision and eventually be able to think like you. You shouldn't have to stop them from being themselves to be effective in your inner circle. Diversity helps an organization. Negativity hurts an organization. Dissention hurts an organization. Disunity hurts an organization but having diverse people with diverse backgrounds can actually help an organization. Diversity is more than just race, gender or age. Diversity includes experience, knowledge, culture and

## Audience/Ideal Client

Once you know what your message is and how you want to help people, you have to know who wants what you have to offer? Who is your target audience? In essence, who wants; and more importantly, who has the means to actually buy what you have to sell? There are people who need what you have to offer, but don't have the money to buy it. There are other people who have the money to buy what you are selling but don't want what you have to sell. The purpose is to find people with both the money and desire to buy what you have to offer. So what is your customer's book topic or genre? What do they do that is directly associated with that book? Where do they hang out on social media in their free time? Initially in business; I didn't know any better. I said that anybody and everybody who wanted to write a book was my customer; but 10 years later, that is not true. I'm different. The marketplace, technology and the publishing industry is different and requires everything from my systems to my customer to be approached differently. Over time, my ideal customer/client/author looks different. I am grateful for all of the referrals, support, great feedback and recommendations that I have received over the years, but I still know exactly who my ideal client is and want it to be. Do you know your customer? Do you hang out with your customer or even know where they hang out? My friend Vanessa Collins and I used to say this often, "It's not that there aren't people out who need and want what we have, but we are in the wrong room with people who don't want to buy what we sell." Sometimes you have to change rooms, neighborhoods, platforms and regions of the planet to get the results and meet the people who need and want your services. Is your book, business and product worth it? Mine is worth it, and so is yours. I am willing to get out of my own way and get in places where my clients are located to do business. Period. Nothing less or nothing more. Let's move forward and do business by finding and building a relationship with our ideal client.

## Consultant/Contractors

In addition to an inner circle, I had to start partnering with and acquiring the services of other contractors. When I started my publishing company, I started out doing everything, but editing. I didn't feel confident doing editing, so I had someone do the one thing that I didn't do well. Over time, I would compare my cover designs to others and realize that I didn't like the cover, so my readers probably didn't like them either. I began hiring graphic designers for covers. Then I hired people to convert my books from paper to eBook. I now have editors, formatters, graphic designers for covers, graphic designers for promotional materials, photographers for photoshoots for custom covers, videographers for my videos and creative director for styling and author development. There are times that I need a graphic designed quickly; but most of the time, I have others who are able to do high-quality work for my clients. Again, I didn't start out that way and you may not be able to do that either. Get the prices and determine the contractors that you want to work with. Make sure that your budget will allow it. I respect people's gifts, talents and time. I don't look for the hookup. If you give me a price, and I don't have the budget for it, I'll say, "I don't have the budget for that." Nothing personal just business. If I still want that person's services, I will pay their price or find someone else who will. My first advice is to watch the person's work. Reach out and ask for a price list upfront. If you are doing business with this person or company, it is not free. Sign a contract along with a proposal that outlines exactly what services you will receive, how much you will have to pay as well as when and how the services will be delivered. If you have questions, be sure to get them answered before you sign the contract or pay for the services.

Another thing to realize is that once you budget for others to do some of the routine work for you, you will have more time to think, plan and prepare for the next moves of your book and business. So start thinking about what services that you could really use the help with your book or business?

## Volunteer Street Team

There are times that you don't need paid help as much as you need people to spread the word about your book or business. A volunteer street team is just that, voices, bodies and connections to spread the word about your book or business. You may need help with registration at a live event, passing out papers, flyers or postcards at an event or just making or returning phone calls. Whatever the task, start compiling a list of people who have said, "If you need help, let me know." Well, be sure and take them up on their offer, but be sure and give them something in appreciation in return for their help. A small gift, an appreciation dinner and a movie or a free entry to one of your events or courses. In some tangible way say, 'Thank you.' Take no one for granted. And if you can return the favor for an event or project of one of your volunteers, be sure to do that. Earlier, I told you how important relationships are to your book and business. Whether the person is being paid or not, it should matter how they are being treated to help you move your book and business message forward. Be honest as to whether you can pay or not but above all be appreciative, humble and grateful for the paid or volunteer help that comes your way.

## Reflection: Who is on Your Dream Team?

# The Action Plan

Now that you've been given so much information, where do you start? I've been asked the same question many times before about writing books and I'm sure that you are concerned about where to start when taking your book to a business. The following are five steps that I encourage you to begin. If you need help with any of the steps, need additional information or advice for any of the steps, reach out to us at http://bit.ly/talkwithroyston or email us at bkroystonpublishing@gmail.com or julia@bkroystonpublishing.com

**Step 1 - Start with You.** I'm not trying to scare you, but I want to be as honest with you as possible. Take inventory of yourself, your attitudes, mentality and discipline. It will take a positive attitude, mental tenacity and drive to succeed in writing, publishing and promoting a book as well as creating a business based on your book. A real hard look and evaluation of the status of your life and the people that you have surrounded yourself will be key to your success as well. Be honest, can those people even handle your success? Be honest with yourself. Have those people been exposed to a level of success in their own lives that would let them be okay with success in your life? You may have to make some changes there first before the book, business or any other endeavor in your life.

What state is my life in right now? What is going great? What needs to be fixed? Who in your life that is good for you to move forward? Who is your life is just not good for you to move forward with a book or a business? Be Honest.

What do you really need? Is it money, people, contacts or an opportunity?

**Step 2 - What is the Message?** What message do you want to deliver to what people?

Who are you talking to? Who are the people that you need to get next to that need the message that you are attempting to deliver

Who do you want to reach?

Where do they hang out?

Are you considered an expert on the topic that your book is about? If not, become an expert as fast as possible.

**Step 3 - Determine and create products and services.** What is the book going to be about? What is the book going to look like so that it attracts the people that you want to buy it and be impacted by it? Visualize your product.

Even if you don't have a title, what does the cover look like? Ask people if they get what you are trying to convey with the product cover that you are possibly going to have someone design. Don't think about what you like first, think about who you are writing the book for and will deliver the message to.

What is the book's title? Is the title related to the message?

What does the cover look like? Does the cover make sense to anyone else but you?

What does your picture look like on the back cover of the book? Does the picture make sense to anyone else but you? Does it look professional?

## Step 4 - Marketing and Promotion

What marketing and promotional outlets are you going to use to get to your audience? Social media? Physical advertisement or old school advertising? Business Cards. Postcards. Vendor Events. Live Events. Live Streaming. Videos. Audios. Conferences. Retreats. Workshops. Courses. Email Marketing Services.

## Step 5 - Developing Systems

The three primary systems are a connection system, payment system and a follow-up system. There are more systems listed in the book but focus on these three. A way for people to connect with you. Email? Website? Social Media? Contact information for people to call you, etc.

What is the way that people will pay you? PayPal, Square, Stripe

How will you follow-up with or communicate with people on a weekly, monthly, quarterly, bi-annual or annual basis?

## Step 6 – Your Dream Team

After some thought and great consideration, who is on your dream team? How can they help the message of your book and ultimately your business get to the world?

Make 3 columns on a piece of paper. Column 1 - People who will be doing the work.

Column 2 - People who will help you spread the word about the work.

Column 3 - People who are your partners whether doing the work, marketing the work or mentoring you to succeed with the work of the book and business.

**Step 7 – Customer Service**

Once of the hardest lessons I have had to learn is what do I do when someone is unhappy or not satisfied with my business' work? Other people are thrilled about my work but there will be customers that are just not satisfied. In business, you will not always satisfy everyone. So here are three things. First, don't ignore them. Second, respond to the concern. Third, take action to amend or rectify the problem quickly and finally, if they are still not satisfied, redo, replace and/or refund. Do your best to make the client happy within reason of your business practices and your contract.

**Reflection:** What are your action steps?

_____
_____
_____
_____
_____
_____
_____
_____
_____
_____
_____
_____
_____
_____
_____
_____
_____
_____
_____
_____

## Lessons Learned

"Always have something that you something well enough that you can charge for it." -Dr. Jack C. Foree. I have since added this, so be sure to have a dollar amount in mind. If not, make one up. After you start doing the work, you will find out whether that dollar amount was too small or too large or just right. In the end, have an amount to start with.

People will take advantage of you if you let them, but don't let them. I learned this the hard way and have been amazed at the people that will take the most advantage. That is a topic for another book and not this book right here. Realize that there are people out there that will take advantage of you and/or try to make you reduce your prices, low ball you or try to get away with demanding a lot for free, but don't let them.  You have to train people on how to treat you.

Intellectual Property - Protect what's yours - Constantly Create - Constantly be creating products and services for people to purchase and be benefited by.  Be sure that you protect what's yours by taking the time to complete copyright applications consistently.  There are pirates out there ready to claim what they didn't create and make a mint off of it.

Be willing to hustle.  Success on any level takes work.  Be willing to put in the work to receive the rewards.  There are those people that don't want to work at all, but stand by and criticize, hate or get jealous of your accomplishments no matter what they are.  These people usually don't have something of their own that they are constantly working on because they would know how hard it is and pray for you instead of talk about you.

Be careful who you pick for your team, but know that you need a team to get further, faster to your goals. This has been the hardest lesson for me. I love people but have trouble trusting that they will do the job as well or as efficiently as I will. I'm not saying I'm perfect or do all things perfectly, but I have a spirit of excellence and want those around me to have that same spirit as well. As I've gotten older, I realize that I could so much more with others helping me. The tired feeling in my body has told me on several occasions, 'Trust somebody and get some help.' I've been disappointed several times, but have learned that I have to be more careful. I MUST interview more thoroughly as well as be as specific as to the tasks I want to be completed as well as how I want them completed in. It has helped me tremendously with my expectations and satisfaction with those who are my team. Go team Go!

Everyone didn't learn to say, 'Thank you, please and that they appreciate you.' If they don't, don't take it personally. Smile at your own accomplishment and learn how to show yourself appreciation.

You need boundaries, limits or a frame in which to work and provide services.

If you're not a risk taker, become a risk taker. Make calculated, well thought out and fully informed risk but take the risk just the same. Nothing risked, nothing rewarded.

The green-eyed monster of jealousy will be a sign that you are on the right path.

Know your industry and the players in the game. Be competitive, but don't compare your skills to someone else's unless it is to make you better. Jealousy is sneaky and will seek to drain your creative energy.

Bonus - Create, Have a Goal, Promote and Launch! (Repeat)

Make sure your links work. It's a matter of money or no money.

Expertise +Availability +Price List = Profitability

Don't wait another minute. Start where you start, mistakes and all, not enough help or not everything in place, just start. You can make it better as you go or next time but just start. Waiting until everything is perfect will most likely never happen and will more likely, delay the inevitable; nothing.

Publishing is a Product as well as Service related industry. If you don't like people, providing customer service and understanding that the book is the Author's baby, Publishing may not be the field, industry or business for you.

**Reflection**: Steps to Turning your Book into a Business

## **About the Author**

Julia Royston is an author, publisher, speaker, teacher and songwriter residing in Southern Indiana with her husband, Brian K. Royston. Julia's motto is "motivating you to be all that you can be, helping you get your message to the masses and turn your words into wealth." She further states that "people hire me to publish their Book, Coach them to write their Book, Provide Ways to promote their Message to the World and Create Products and Services surrounding their Book." Julia has written more than 45 books, published and coached 100+ authors to release 150+ books. Prior to full-time publishing and coaching, Julia spent 22 years as a certified, media specialist/technology instructor in a public and private school system. For more information about Julia and her companies visit, www.juliaroyston.net or www.bkroystonpublishing.com.

To connect with Julia on Social Media

Facebook: www.facebook.com/juliaaroyston

Twitter: @juliaakroyston

Instagram: @jujuroyston

LinkedIN: www.linkedin.com/juliaaroyston

Access these other helpful resources visit,

**100 Ways to be a Book Business Boss**

http://bit.ly/bookbusiness100

**Royston Writer's Package**

http://bit.ly/writeitnow

www.ingramcontent.com/pod-product-compliance
Lightning Source LLC
Chambersburg PA
CBHW071215160426
43196CB00012B/2310